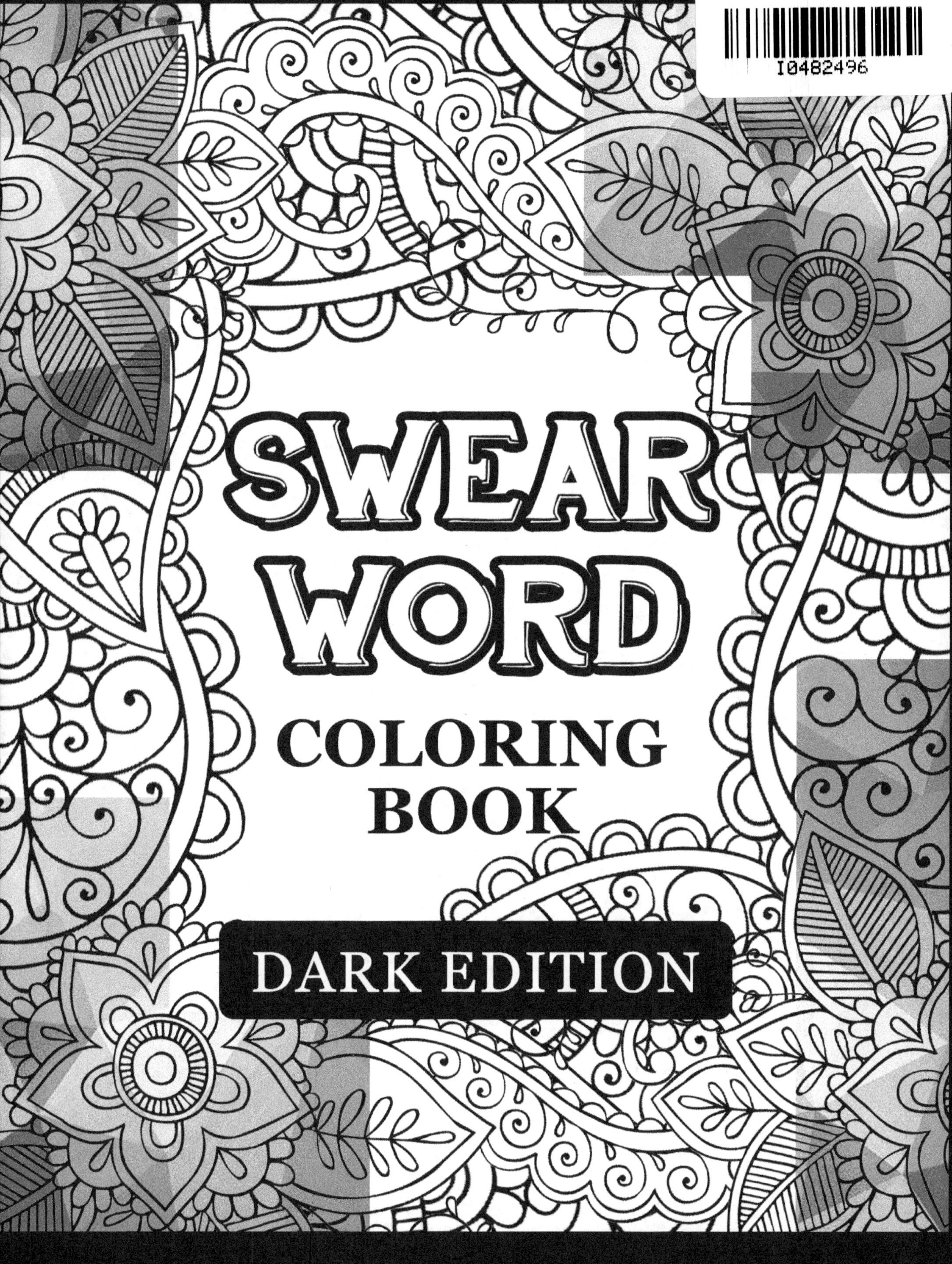

SWEAR WORD

COLORING BOOK

DARK EDITION

COLOR TEST PAGE

COLOR TEST PAGE

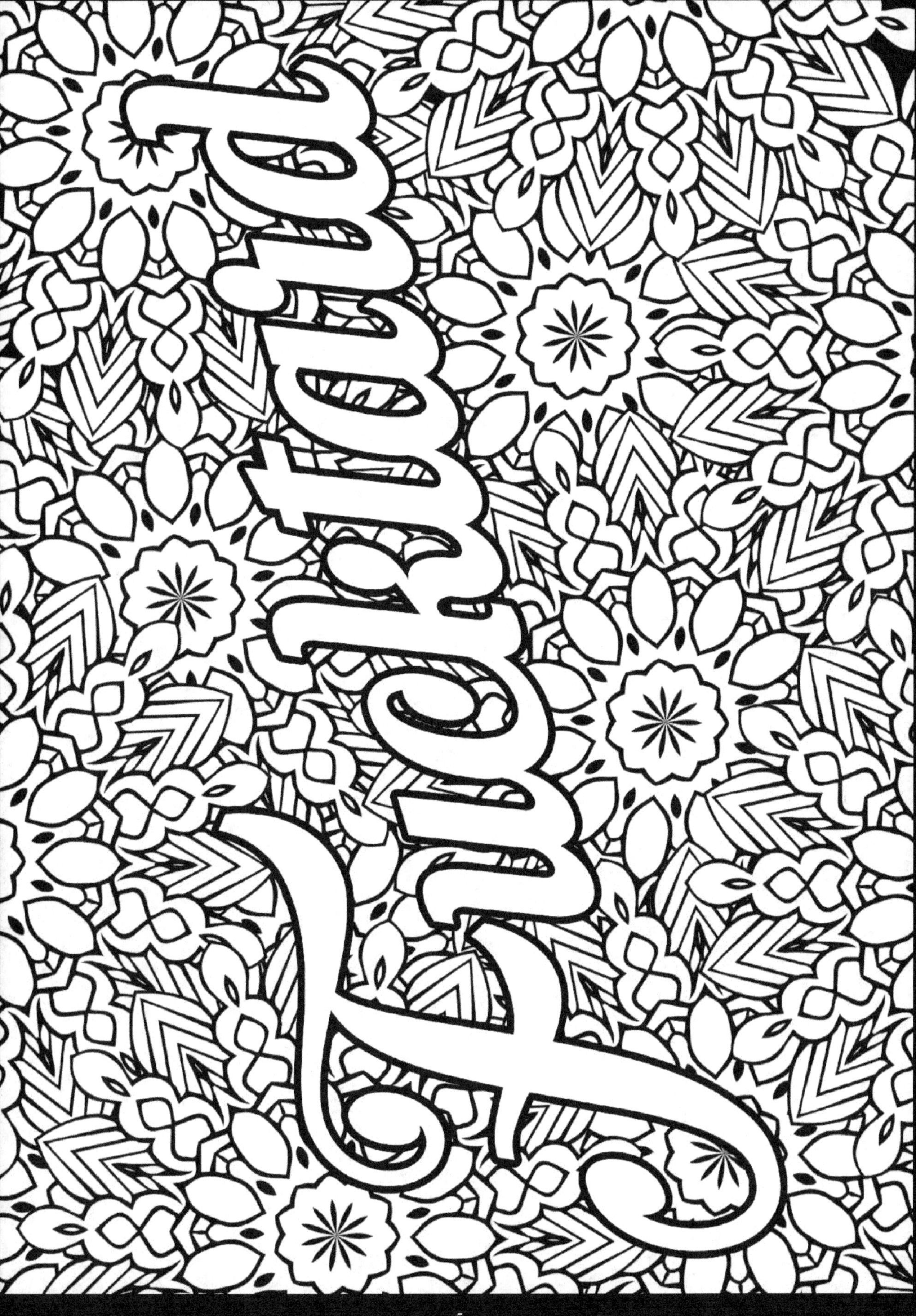
Fucktard

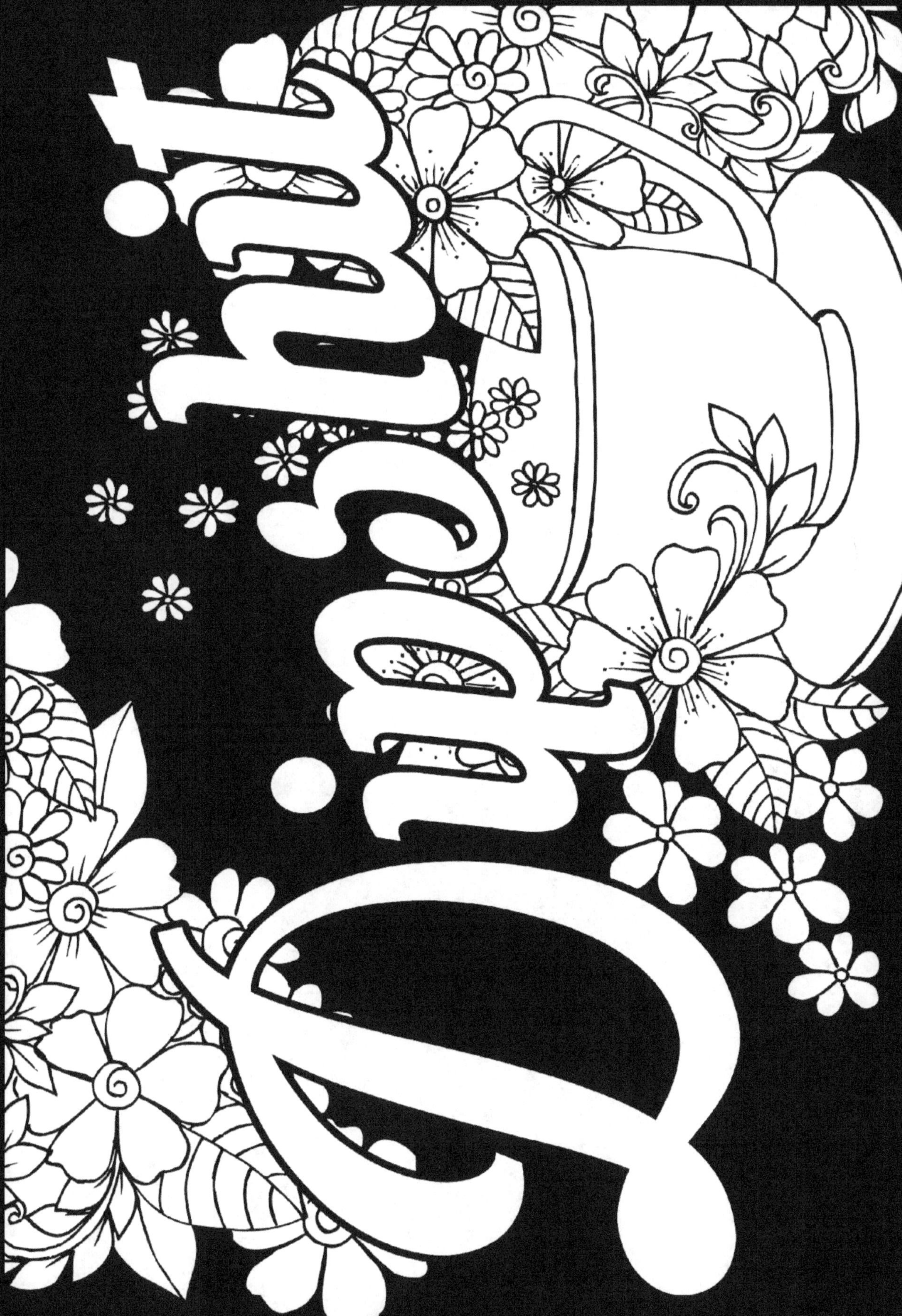
Dipshit

Shit-a-brick

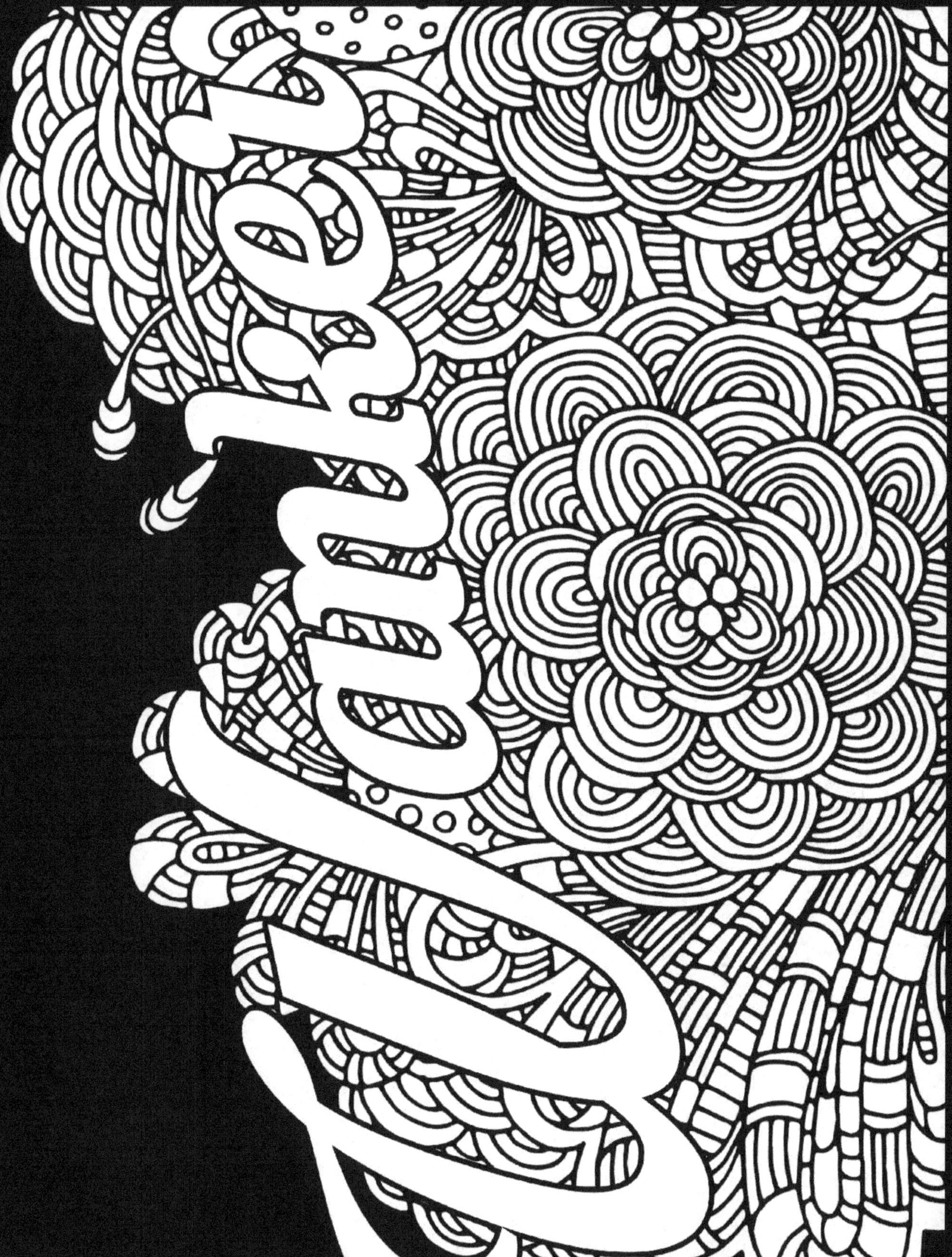
Wanker

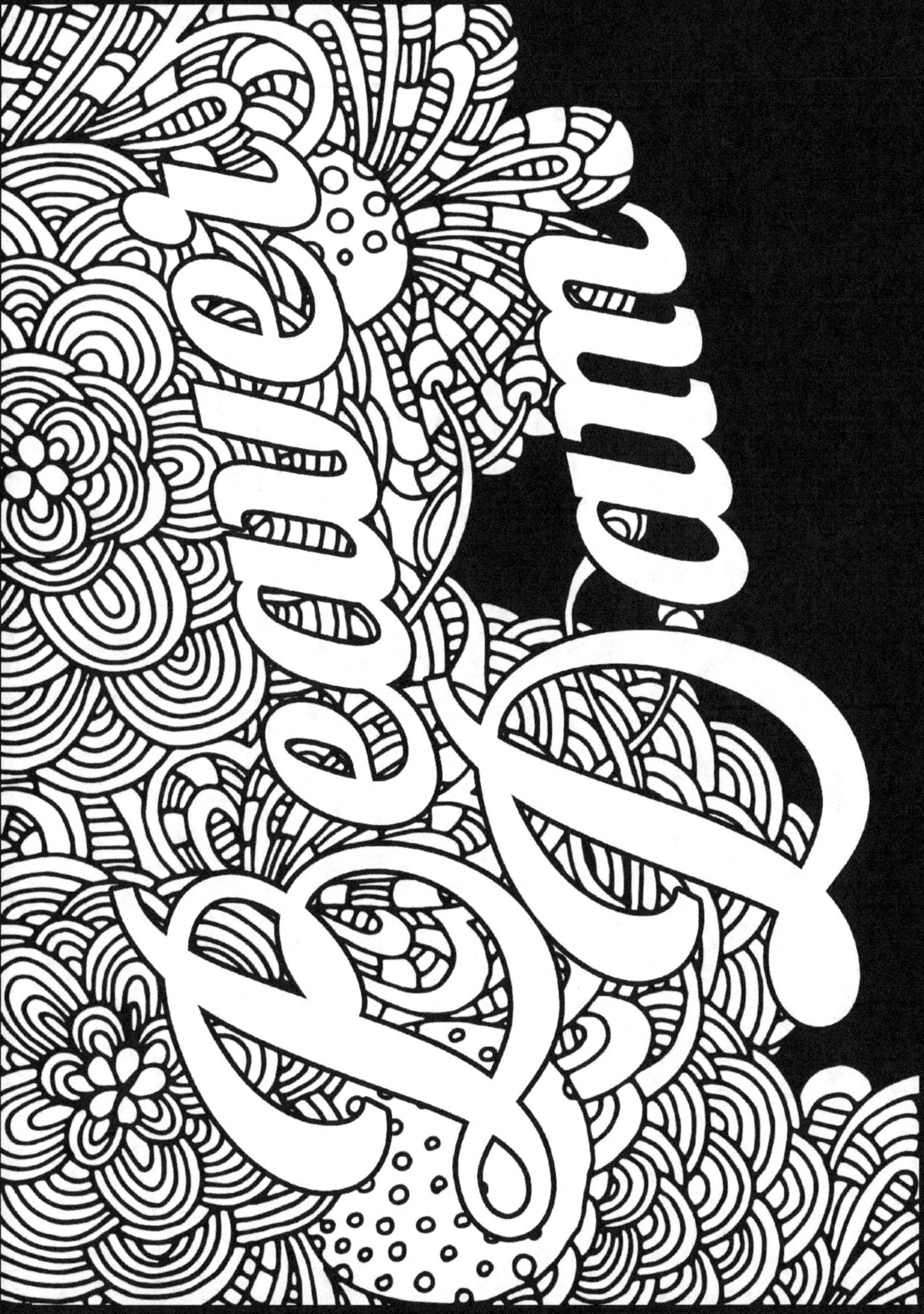
Beaver Dam

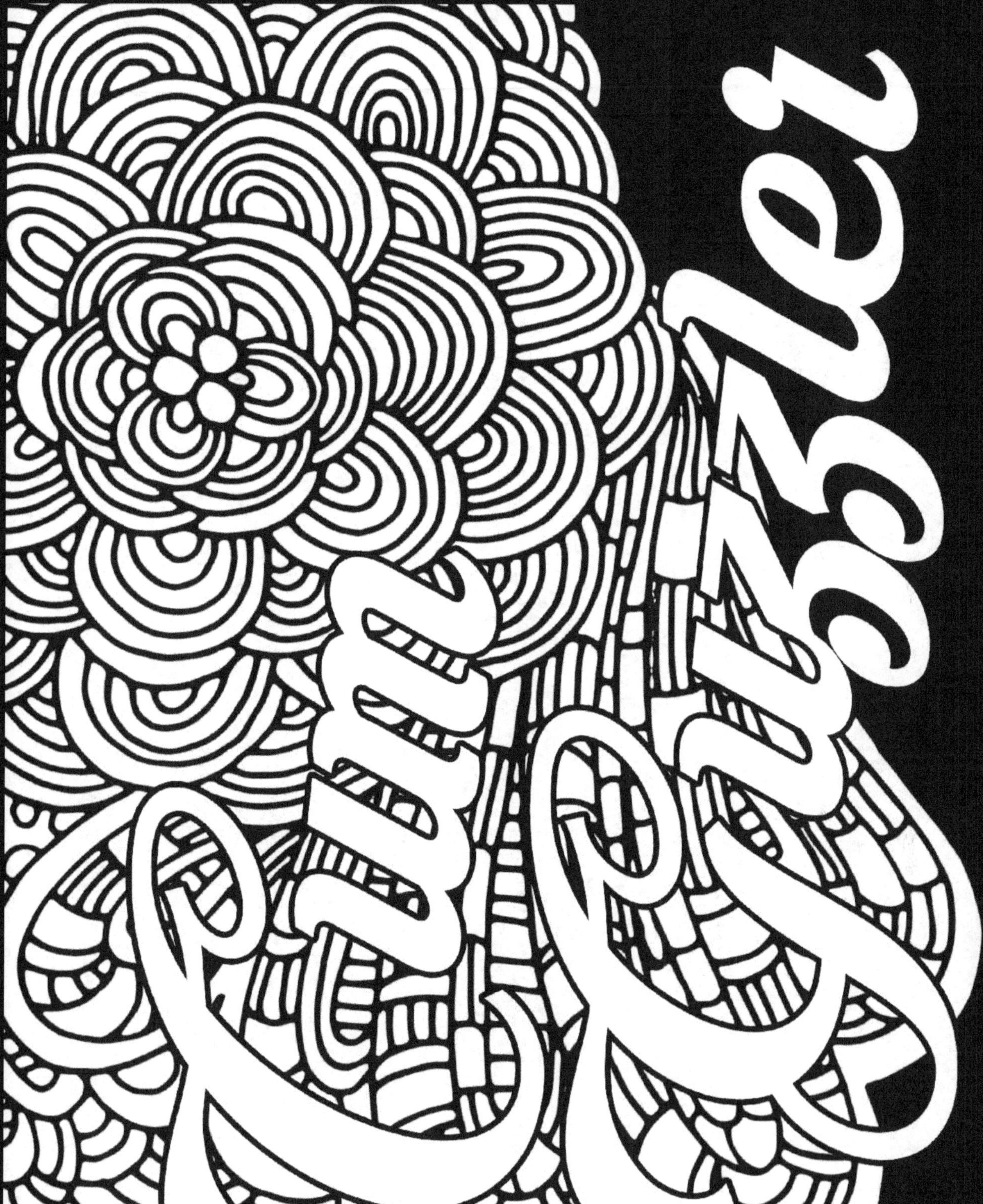
Cum Guzzler

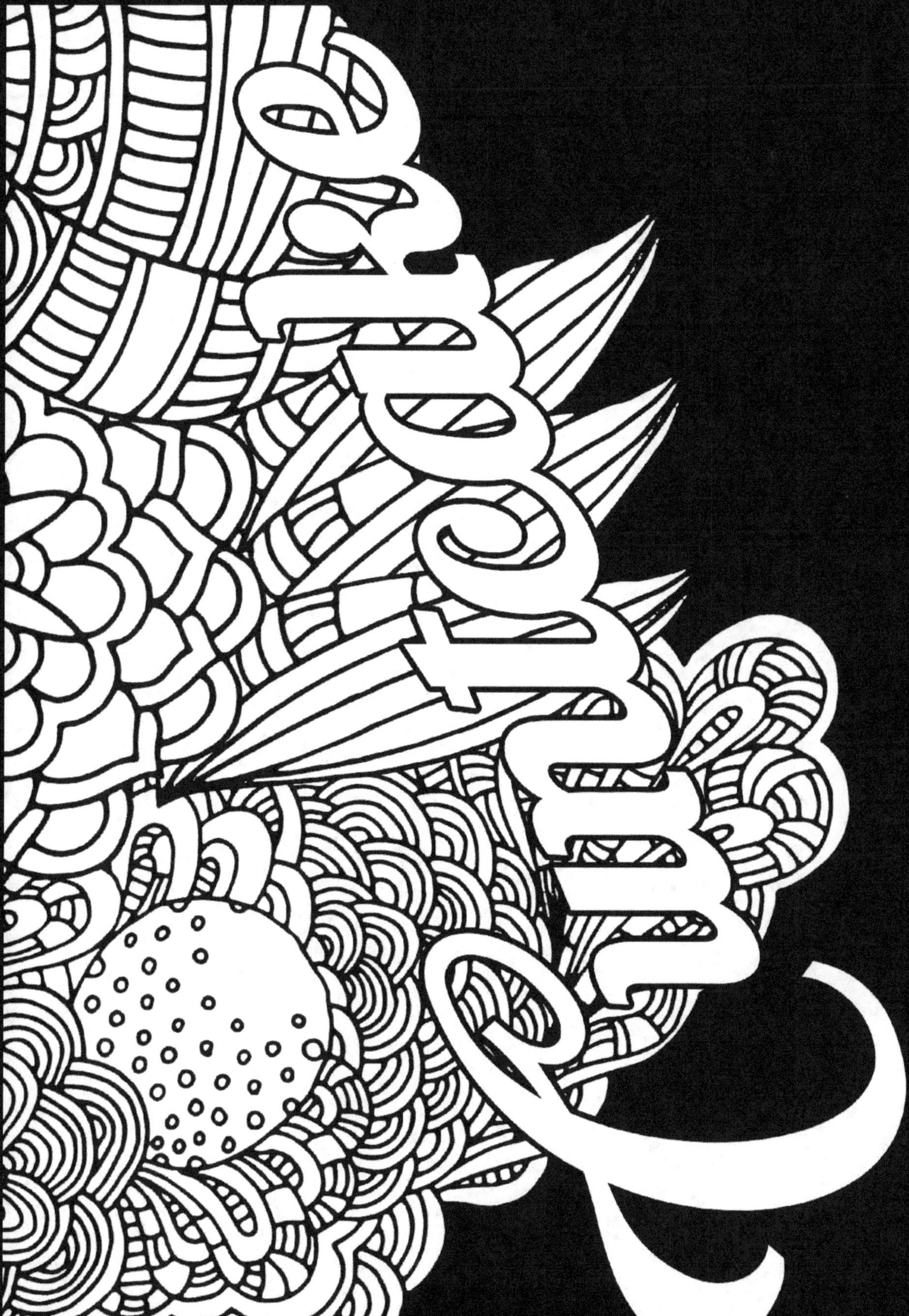
Cuntcake

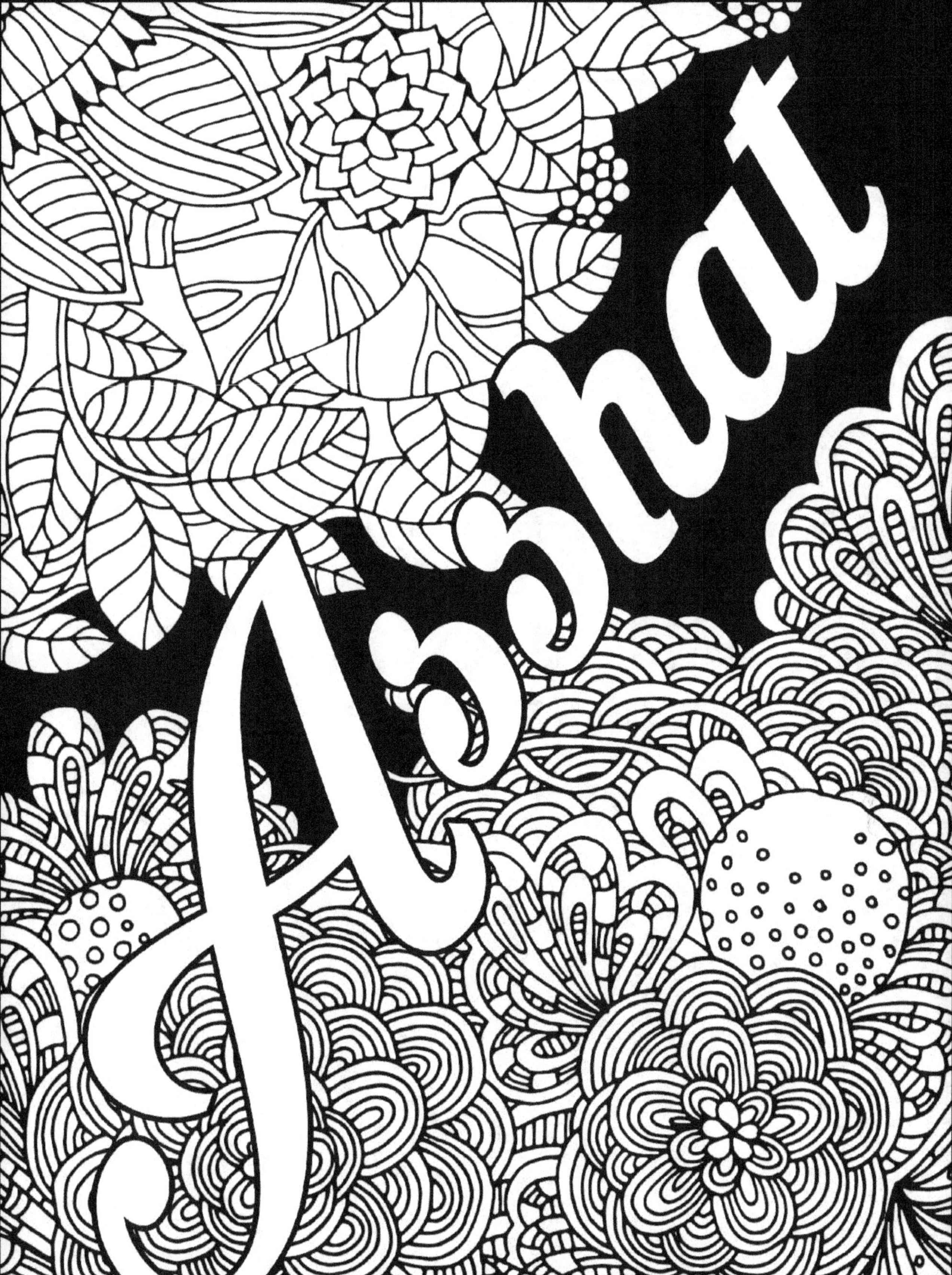
Asshat

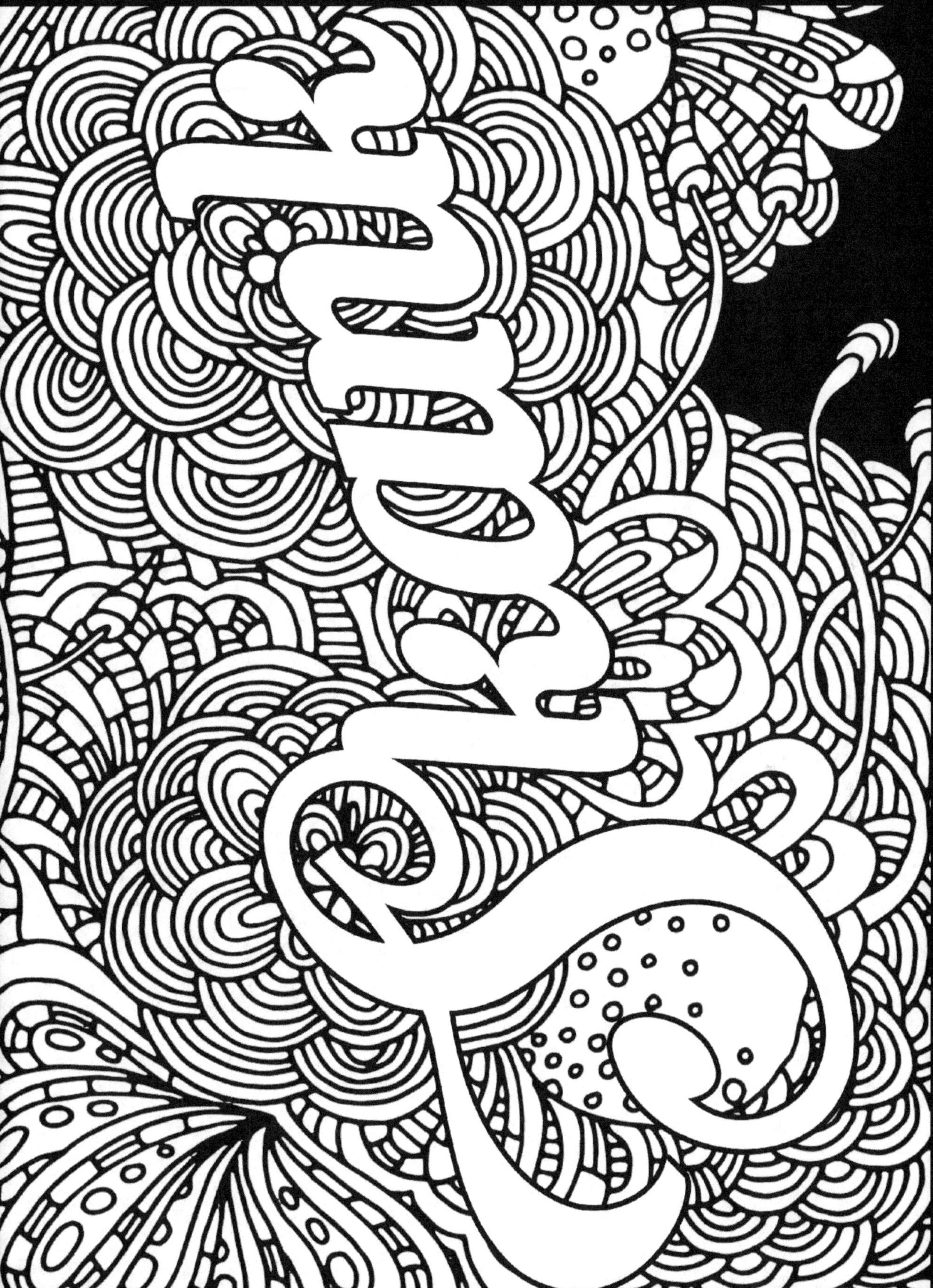
Skank

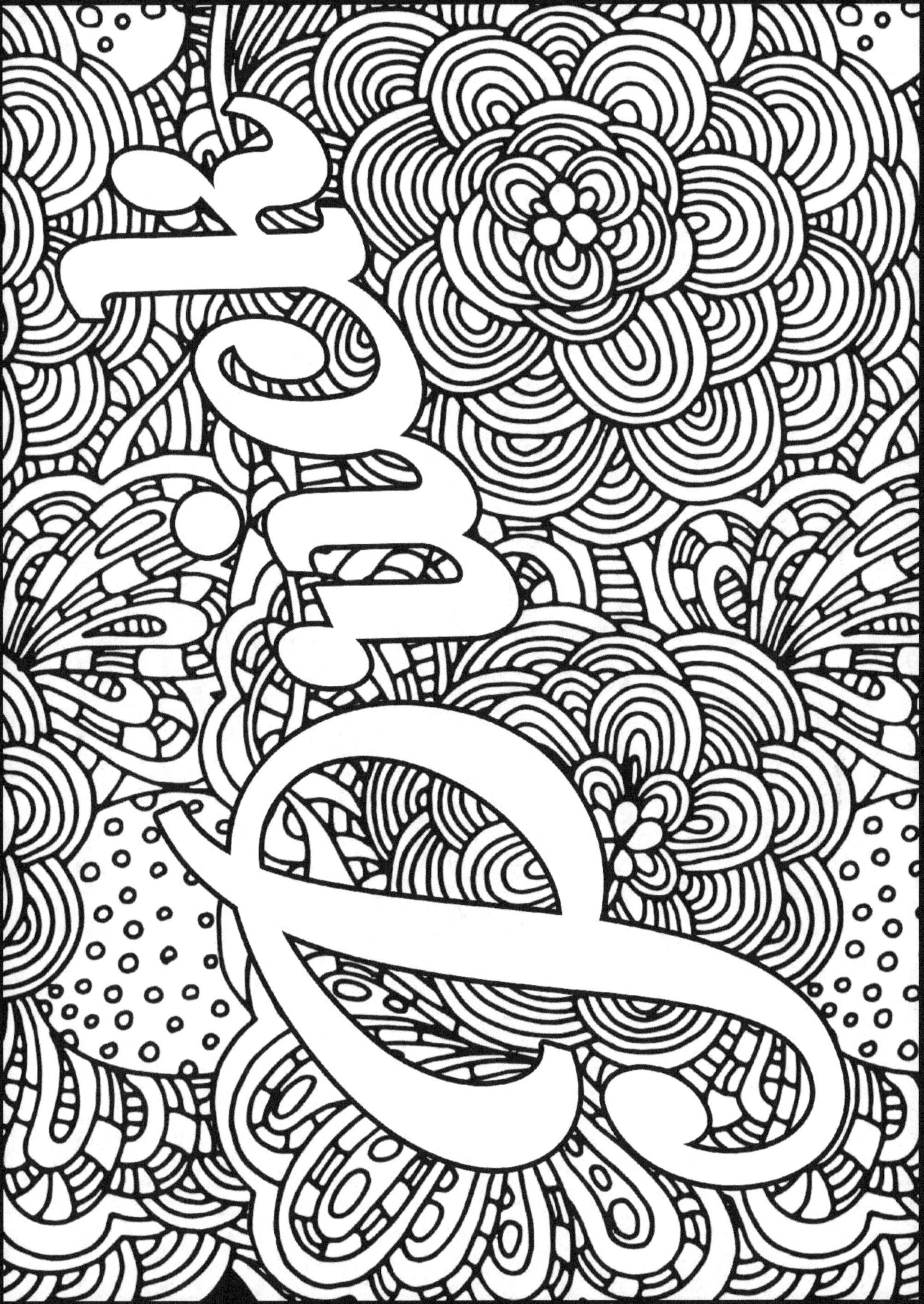
Prick

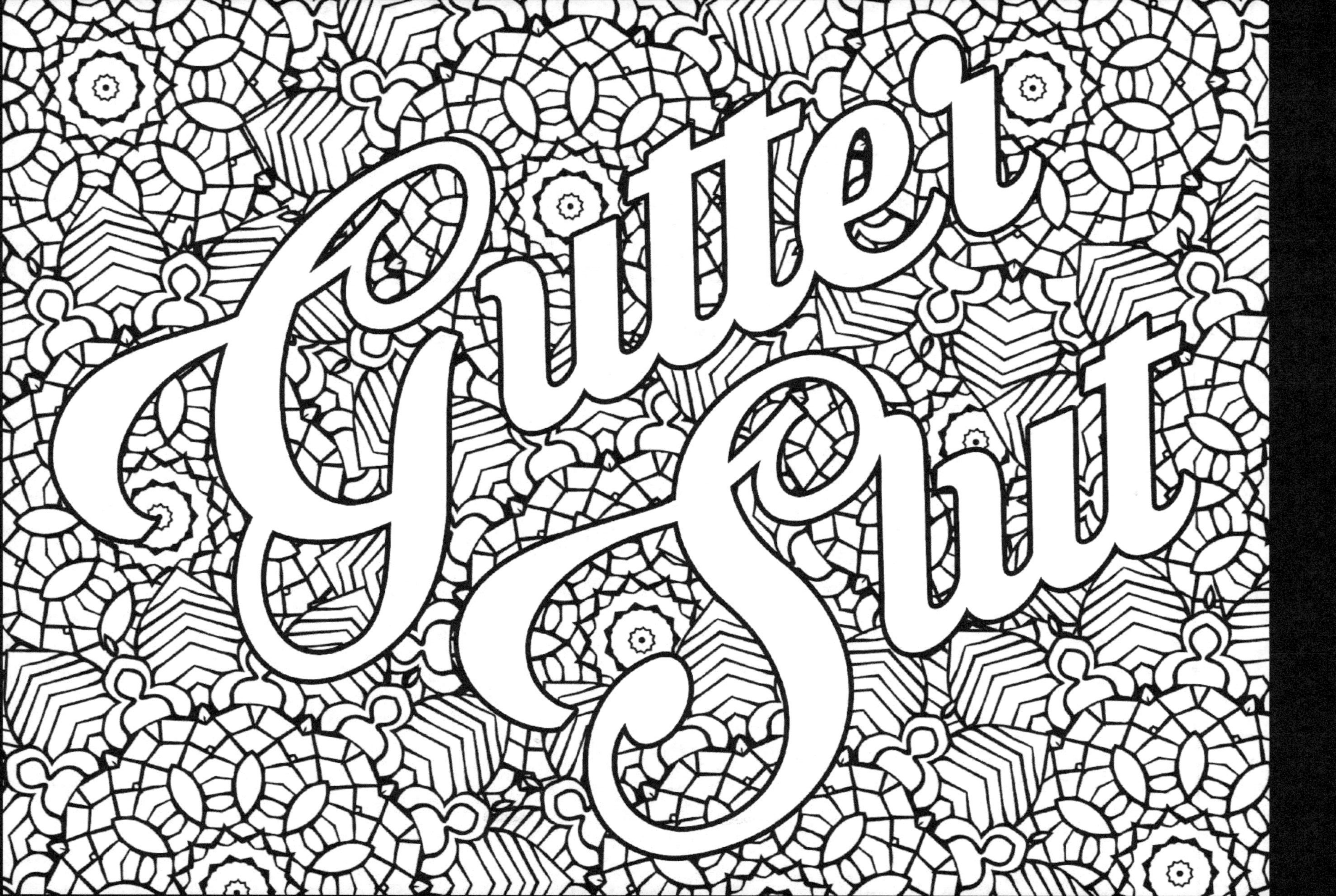
Gutter Slut

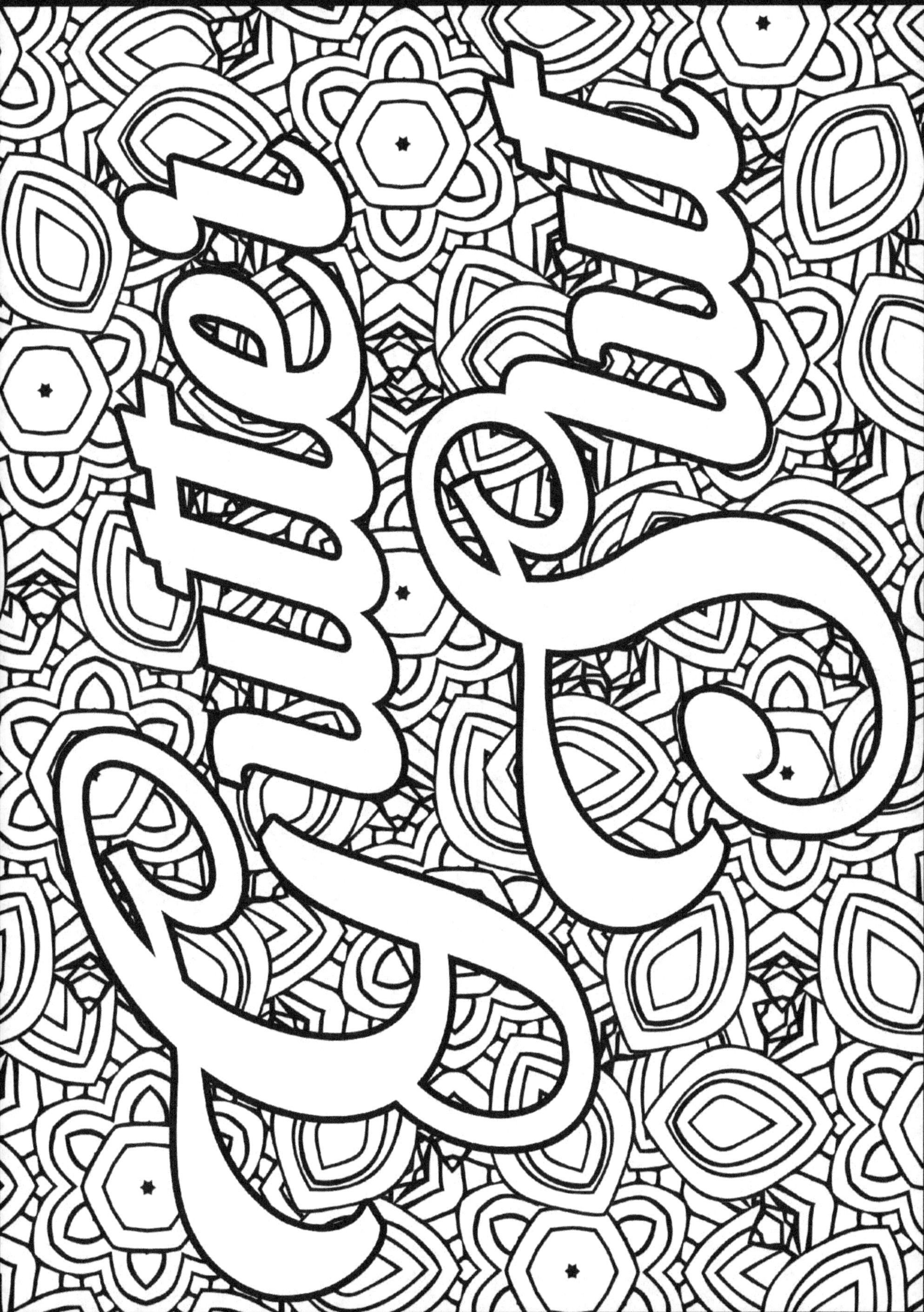
Gutter
Slut

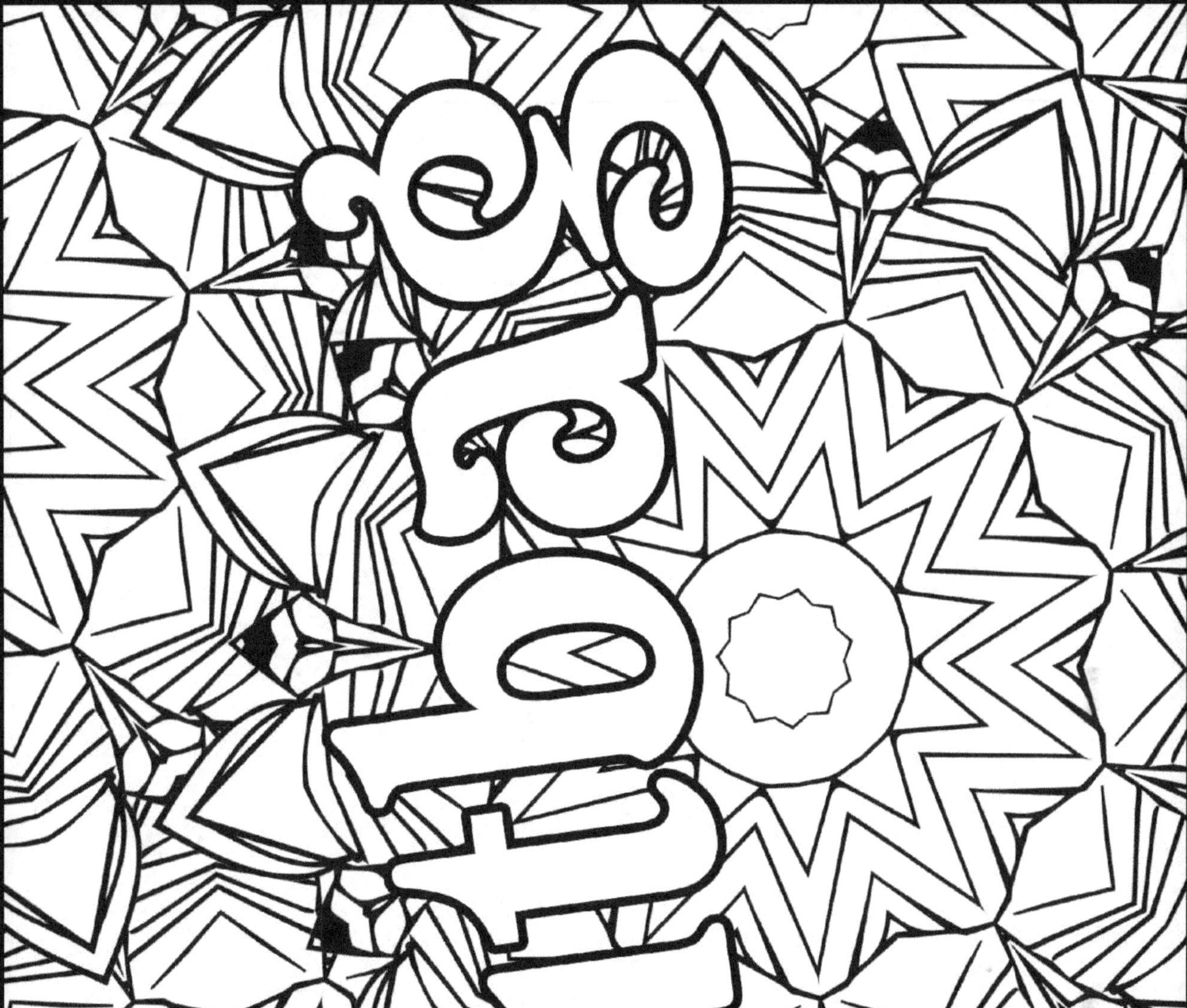
Slutbag

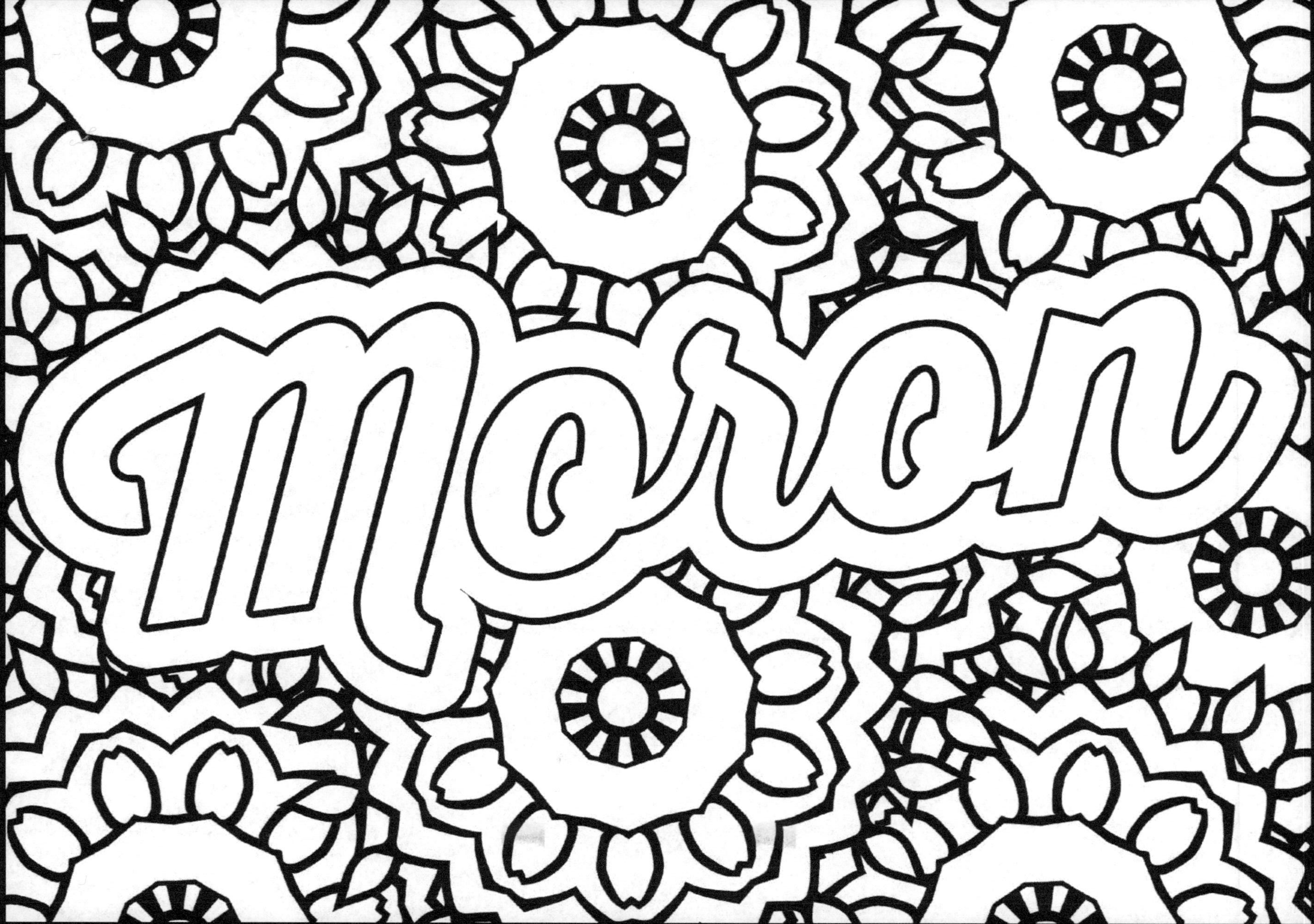
Moron

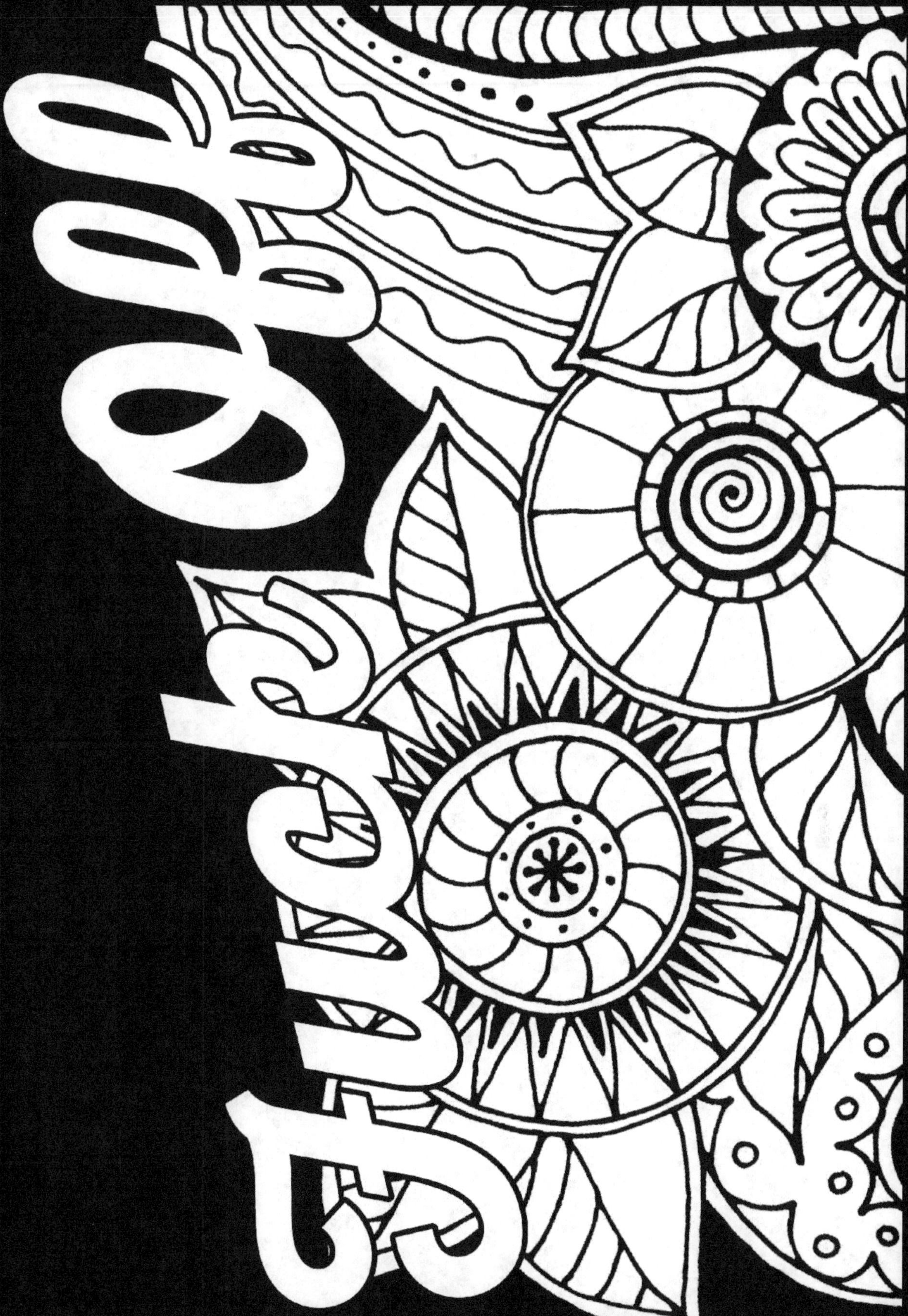
Fuck Off

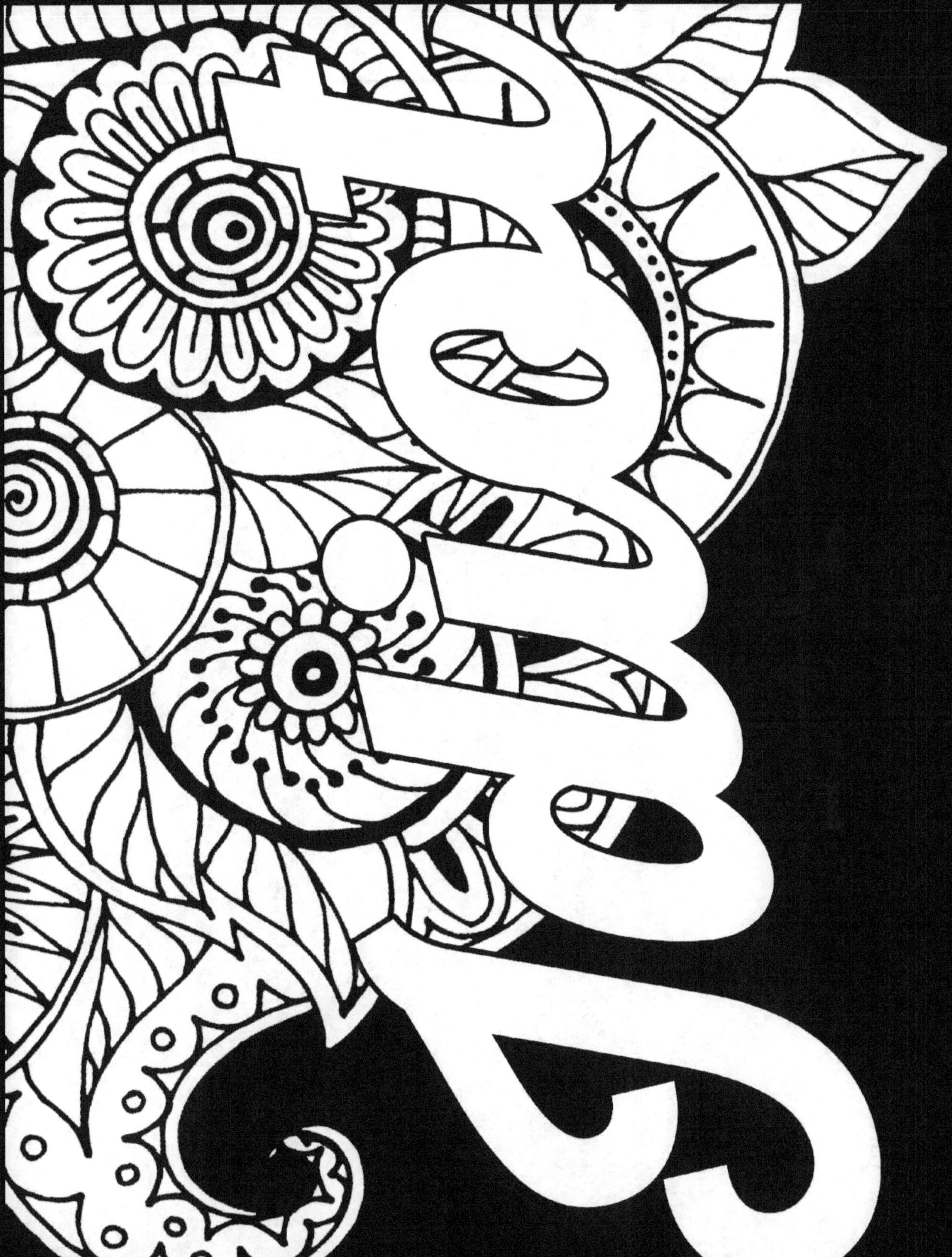
Idiot

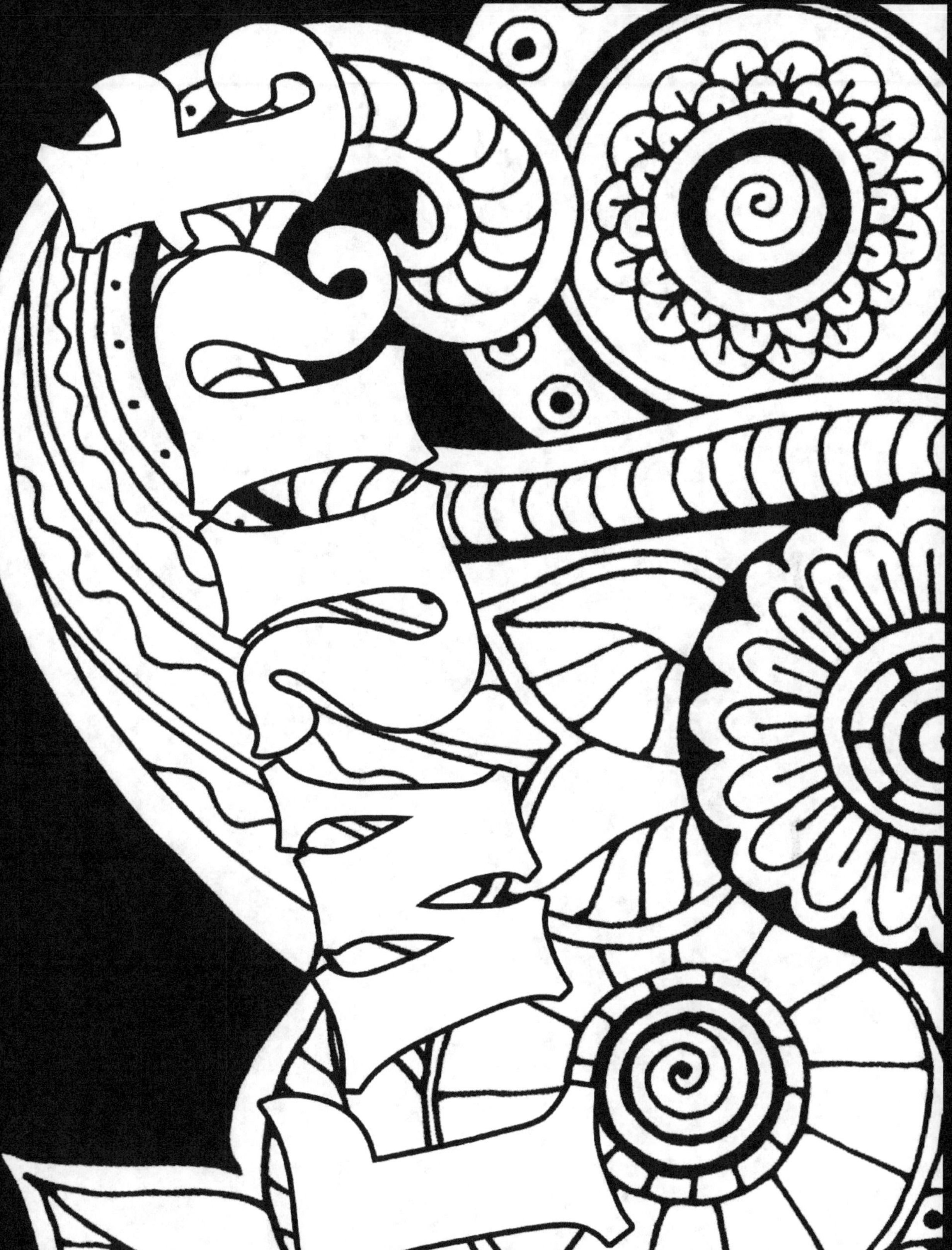

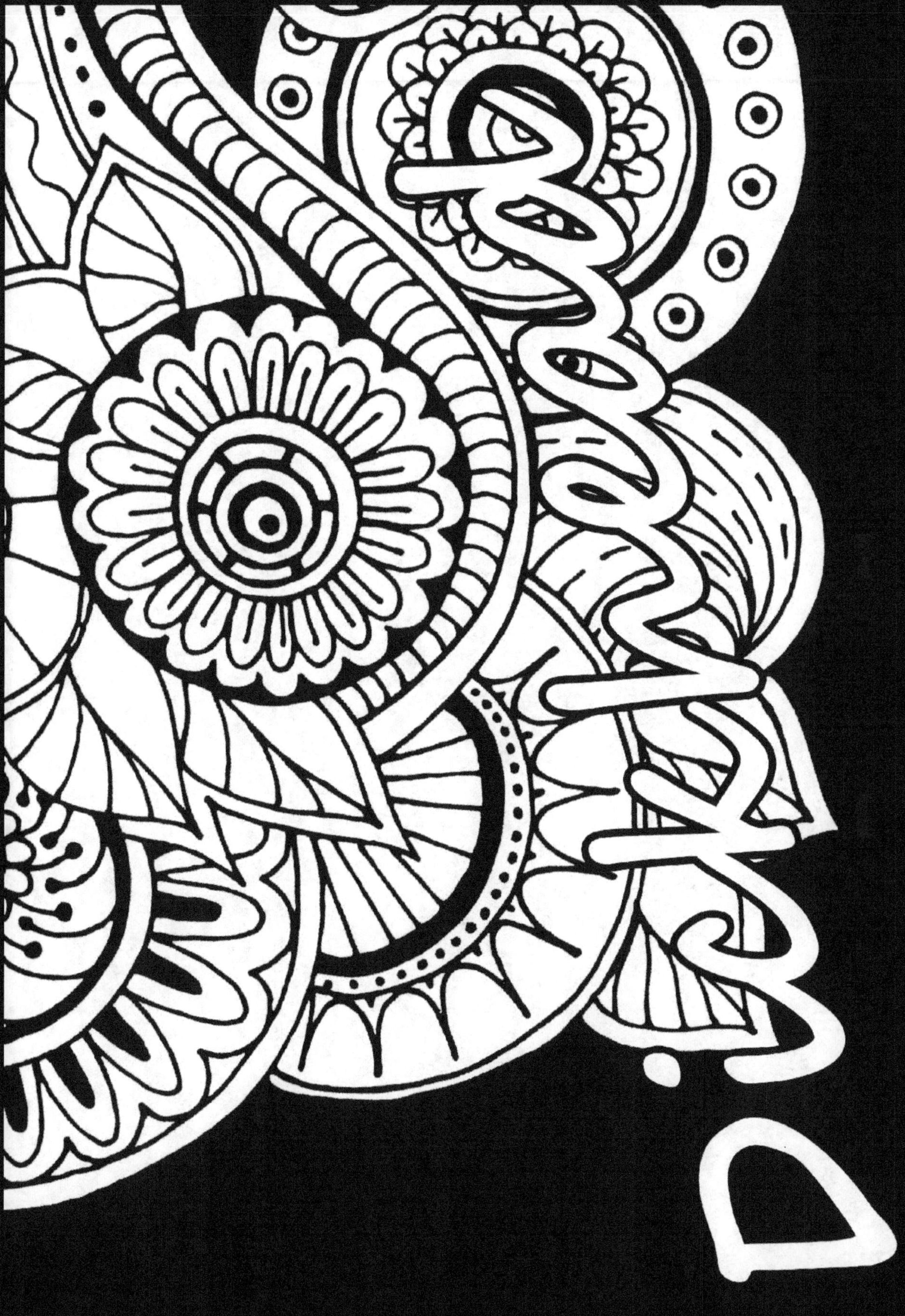
Dickhead

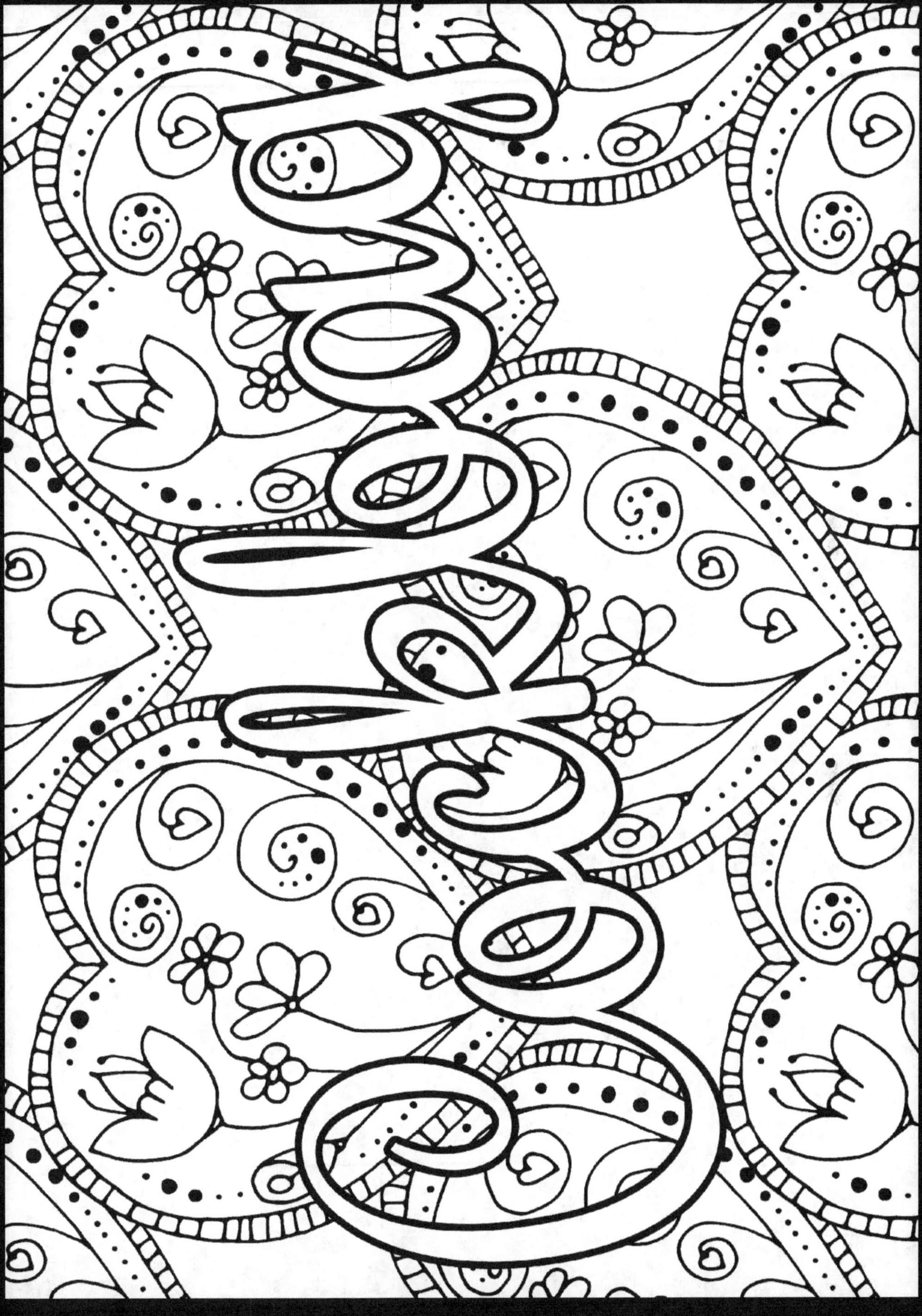
Cockbag

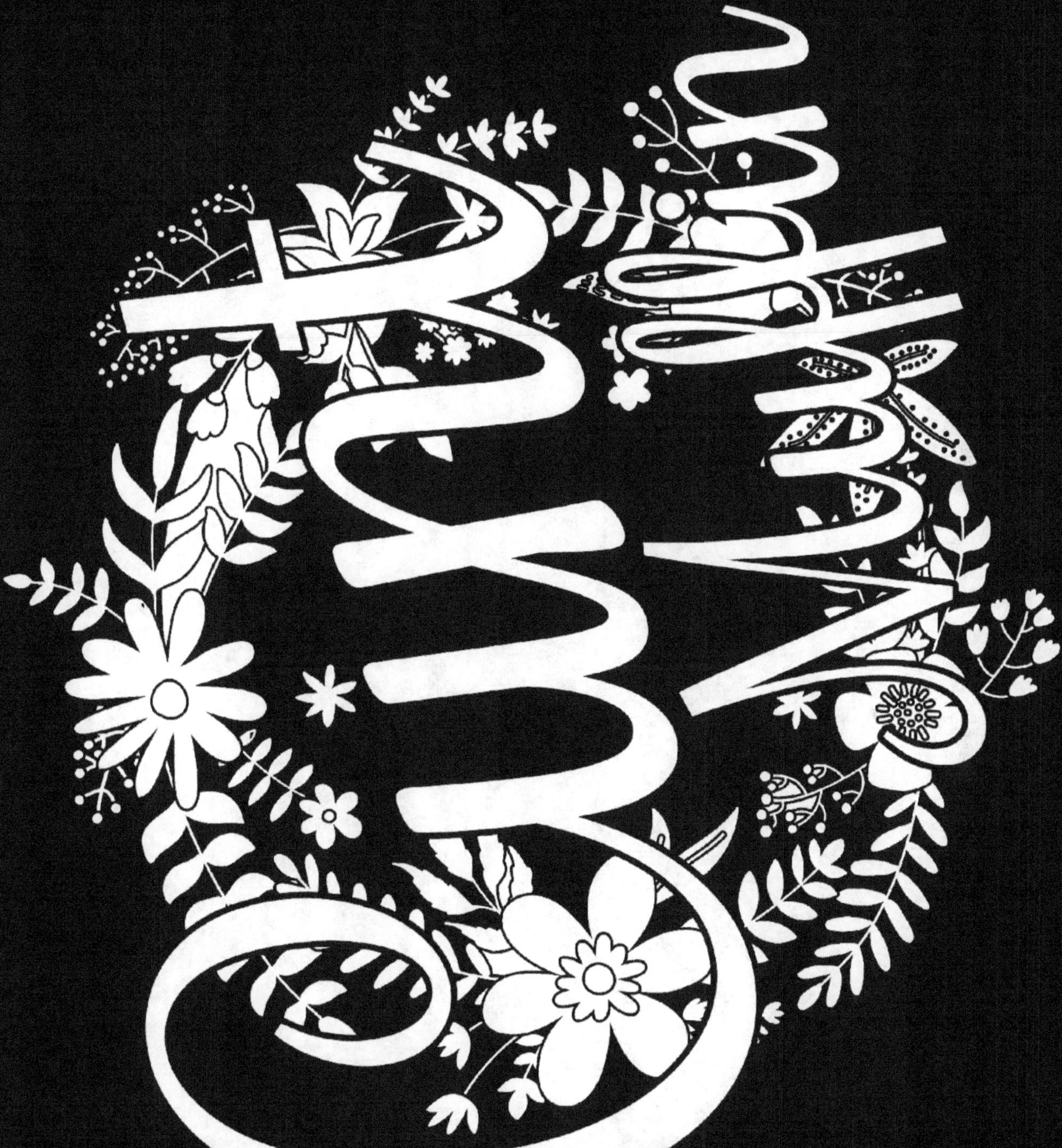
Cunt
Muffin

www.ingramcontent.com/pod-product-compliance
Lightning Source LLC
Chambersburg PA
CBHW080611190526
45169CB00007B/2963
* 9 7 8 1 5 3 4 7 7 9 5 1 8 *